somerset

foreword

stunning sea views, a charming rural setting, steeped in history...

Writing a sales listing for Somerset would be an easy task, for the county comes complete with so many attractive features.

From the spectacular Glastonbury Tor, across the Levels to the hustle and bustle of Taunton and on to Exmoor via a host of picturesque market towns and scenic idylls, Somerset truly offers something for everyone.

This year, the County Gazette is marking 180 years of representing the people and places of Somerset.

So it seems apt to document this part of the world now with a photographic journey across our beautiful county.

As an editor, putting together this book has in many ways felt like creating a brochure for our county.

And it is fitting that Wilkie May & Tuckwood, a firm founded in the south west and with such strong roots in the county, has supported the publication.

Equally fitting is that the company is celebrating an anniversary of its own — 25 years providing high-level service to clients.

Putting this book together has been a hugely enjoyable challenge, writing, selecting and editing content which is so rich in subject matter.

Though we have scoured every corner of our county to give readers a glimpse into Somerset, for every single photograph, fact or observation, there are countless more out there we have been unable to feature.

So keep searching yourselves and drop us a line with your photographs and your thoughts

and who knows, there may be a volume two.

For a picture is worth a thousand words — and there are truly thousands to be told about glorious Somerset.

My words could not hope to cover a fraction of the history, scenery and evolution of such an extraordinary county. But the pictures do a fantastic job.

Enjoy your trip.

Paul Jones,
Editor, County Gazette

in association with

WILKIE MAY & TUCKWOOD

www.wilkie.co.uk

Some of the 274 steps that make up Jacob's Ladder at Cheddar Gorge

3

taunton deane

sweeping rural landscapes alongside picturesque, traditional towns and villages

The county town of Taunton lies at the heart of a stunning district, complete with picture-postcard villages and stunning rural vistas.

While Taunton itself boasts a population of around 65,000, the second largest town in the area is Wellington, with around 15,000 residents.

Castle Square sits at the heart of Taunton, with quaint shopping precincts crawling away in every direction, all leading to the River Tone, bisecting the town.

The skyline is dominated by the spires of the churches of St Mary Magdalene, St James and St Gregory, contrasted against the more recent developments such as the recently-renamed Cooper Associates County Ground.

Home of Somerset County Cricket Club, the riverside county ground is ranked among the most picturesque cricketing venues in the country, if not the world, and on a match day adds the sound of leather on willow and the cheers of the crowd to the usual cacophony of a thriving town.

Wellington sits in the shadow of the landmark monument, built in honour of the first Duke of Wellington, Arthur Wellesley.

Surrounding the larger towns is a plethora of picturesque Somerset outposts, such as Combe Florey, Wiveliscombe, Bishops Lydeard and Milverton.

The district also boasts two Areas of Outstanding Natural Beauty, the Blackdown Hills and the Quantocks.

The combination of traditional urban development and stunning rural landscapes in such close proximity gives the area a uniquely picturesque setting and feel.

Residents and visitors are never far from some trademark Somerset scenery and tradition, including the likes of Sheppy's cider, produced near Wellington and a raft of farming, from livestock rearing to fruit growing.

in association with

WILKIE MAY & TUCKWOOD

www.wilkie.co.uk

Taunton's North Town Bridge links the town across the River Tone

The landmark Market House at the heart of Taunton

did you know?

- Taunton was the first town in the country to be lit permanently by electric street lighting in 1881.

- Wellington was the home of Fox, Fowler and Company, the last commercial bank permitted to print its own sterling banknotes in England and Wales.

- The first branch of clothing retailer New Look was opened in Taunton in 1969 by Tom Singh, who lived in Wellington.

- Hestercombe Gardens features three unique gardens, spanning three centuries of history and design.

- Colonel John Chard, who was awarded the Victoria Cross for his part in the defence of Rorke's Drift, died at Hatch Beauchamp in 1897.

- Experiments carried out by Andrew Crosse at Fyne Court, near Taunton, are believed to have inspired Mary Shelley to write Frankenstein.

- The Taunton Flower Show is among the world's oldest, having been first held in 1831.

- Standing at 174ft tall, the Wellington Monument is the tallest three-sided structure in the world. It was started in 1817, but wasn't completed until 1854 due to funding problems and other issues.

- The monument was also originally intended as a plinth for a statue of Arthur Wellesley, but the statue was never made.

- Notable Taunton residents past and present include actress and model Patti Boyd, actress Jenny Agutter, footballer and manager Colin Addison and businesswoman Deborah Meaden.

- The Market House in Taunton was built in 1682.

- Major rebuilding took place in Wellington following a fire in 1731, after which it became a centre for cloth-making.

- Taunton's Vivary Park was, in medieval times, the fish farm - or vivarium - for the town's priory and castle, although there are no visible remains.

Looking through the corn on Blagdon Hill

taunton deane

■ Bath Place, Taunton, is a hive of independent shops (right)

■ Vivary Park offers a town-centre retreat for Tauntonians (below)

St Mary Magdalene Church, in Hammet Street, Taunton (left)

Picture: Paul Jones (bottom right)

The Cooper Associates County Ground in Taunton, home of Somerset County Cricket Club, is ranked among the most picturesque in the country

taunton deane

■ The Willow Cathedral at Longrun Meadow, created out of willow from the Levels (right)

■ The village of Kingston St Mary (top right)

The St Mary the Virgin Church stands proudly in this view of West Buckland

Picture: Geoff Hall (top left)

The entrance to Taunton Castle, now home to the Museum of Somerset

taunton deane

The view at Ford (left)

The Nynehead Hunt rides out (right)

Cows graze before the Wellington Monument (above)

Sheep enjoying the view at Cothelstone Hill

taunton deane

■ Signs at sunset in North Curry
(top right) and Hillfarrance
(bottom right)

Pointing the way at Blagdon Hill

Burrow Mump sits in the distance in Burrowbridge

taunton deane

The Church of St Bartholomew, at East Lyng, stands above flood water in this view from Curload

A gate leading to a corn field and stunning views beyond at Brompton Ralph

taunton deane

- Bales at Wellington (top left)
- Tonedale Mill, near Wellington (left)
- Cygnets hitching a ride on Wellington Basins (right)

Somerset countryside seen from near Wellington (above)

The church ruins atop Burrow Mump, at Burrowbridge, look out across the Levels

sedgemoor

rebellious history, scenic waterways, tourist resorts and industrial heritage

Perhaps most famous as the venue of the final battle of the Monmouth Rebellion, which took place at Westonzoyland in 1685, Sedgemoor has a rich and varied history.

The administrative centre of the district, Bridgwater, is mentioned in the Domesday Book and developed as a trade centre due to its position at the mouth of the River Parrett.

During the Second World War Sedgemoor - primarily Bridgwater - was the target of German bombers. The Bridgwater and Taunton Canal, built in 1827, formed part of the Taunton Stop Line, which was designed to halt the advance of any German invasion. Pillboxes can still be seen along the scenic waterway.

Perhaps the town's most famous son is Robert Blake, regarded as among the most important military commanders of the Commonwealth during the 17th Century.

Born in Bridgwater, he died in 1657 and a statue of him stands at the top of Fore Street.

Sedgemoor is also home to Hinkley Point, a headland on the Bristol Channel, perhaps most famous in recent times as the site of two nuclear power stations; Hinkley Point A and Hinkley Point B. In the autumn of 2016, there were plans to construct a third power station – Hinkley Point C.

Holidaymakers will also be familiar with parts of Sedgemoor. Burnham-on-Sea, Brean and Berrow have become major tourist destinations and the areas form one of the highest concentrations of caravans in Europe.

A stretch of sand between the resorts, which features eight beaches, makes the area a popular location for walkers, sand sailors, wind surfers and sand artists, with Brean Down providing views across the Bristol Channel on one side and over the Somerset Levels on the other.

Stunning landscapes, combined with a rich industrial heritage and some historic British holiday resorts, give Sedgemoor a rare diversity and something for everyone.

in association with

WILKIE MAY & TUCKWOOD

www.wilkie.co.uk

A farmhouse sits in rural splendour in this view across Spaxton

St Margaret's Church, in Spaxton, stands proudly on the horizon

did you know?

■ Brent Knoll Hill, now a popular vantage point with views across the Levels and beyond, was originally home to an Iron Age fort. It stands 449ft above sea level.

■ Serena de la Hey designed and built the 40ft-tall Willow Man, who stands alongside the M5 near Bridgwater, in 2000 and celebrates the role of willow in the Somerset landscape.

■ Cheddar Gorge is one of two in Somerset. The other is Ebbor Gorge.

■ Bridgwater's famous carnival can be traced back to the Gunpowder Plot of 1605, after which King James I and his parliament decreed the events should be commemorated by the lighting of bonfires each year on November 5.

■ The Battle of Sedgemoor, which took place in 1685 at Westonzoyland, was the last pitch battle on English soil.

■ The battle was the final confrontation of the Monmouth Rebellion, which saw the rebel James Scott, the 1st Duke of Monmouth, proclaimed King on the Cornhill in Bridgwater before his forces were defeated.

■ The stretch of sand between Burnham-on-Sea and Brean Down is the second longest in Europe and includes eight beaches.

■ Poet Geoffrey Chaucer was deputy forester at the royal estate of Petherton Park, in North Petherton.

■ The Bridgwater and Taunton Canal, built in 1827, was bought by the Great Western Railway in 1866 and continued to see commercial traffic until 1907.

■ Scenes from the period drama Wolf Hall were filmed on the canal, between Albert Street and West Street near Bridgwater, the iconic beams representing Traitors Gate.

■ In the mid-nineties, Clash Frontman Joe Strummer visited Bridgwater Carnival and declared 'This is a Clash Town, I love this place, I want to live here'. He did.

■ Held every 10 years, the Axbridge Pageant tells the 1000-year story of the town.

■ The oldest complete human skeleton, an estimated 9,000 years old, was found at Cheddar Caves in the Mendip Hills.

The Willow Man sculpture is a popular landmark in the South West

The Old Church of St Nicholas, in Uphill, stands atop a cliff overlooking Brean Down and the mouth of the River Axe

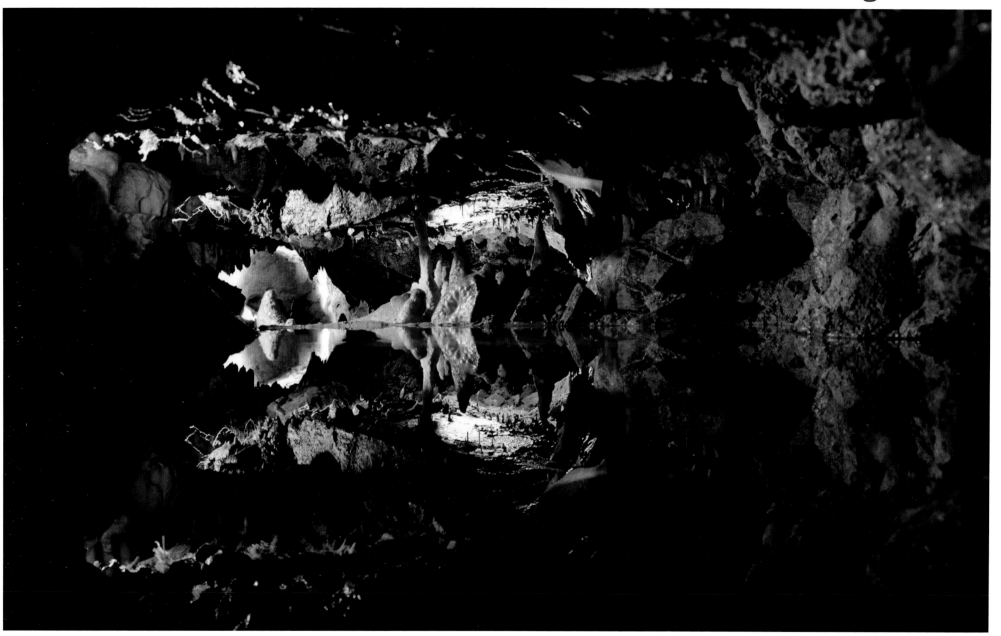

Britain's oldest complete human skeleton, dated at around 9,000 years old, was found in the caves at Cheddar

Cheddar sits in England's largest gorge and offers spectacular caving

Cheddar Gorge attracts around 500,000 visitors each year

Bridgwater's Corn Exchange and Market Hall, above, and the statue of Robert Blake which stands outside (right)

The unique act of squibbing, when scores of people set off fireworks simultaneously, signals the end of the Bridgwater Carnival celebrations each year

sedgemoor

Cygents (right) and livestock enjoying Mark Moor in the shadow of the Glastonbury Tor (far right)

The man-made River Huntspill at West Huntspill

Picture: Andrew Linthorne (top left)

A horse strolls on Brent Knoll

sedgemoor

■ The Axbridge Drug Store
(top and bottom right)

The town boasts a wealth of half-timbered buildings, including King John's Hunting Lodge (main image)

St John's Church, Axbridge, which dates from the 13th Century

sedgemoor

Burnham-on-Sea's scenic yacht harbour (top), landmark wooden lighthouse (right) and pier at low tide (above)

Picture: Peter Diment (right)

The beach at Burnham-on-Sea at sunset

north somerset

sandy beaches, a modern pier, tourist hotspots and tucked-away villages

North Somerset, although an important hub in the county, is run by a unitary authority and has an independent feel.

It covers the north west of the county, although a government plan to name the district as such was dismissed in 1996 and the title North Somerset adopted.

With Bristol to the north, Bath to the east and the Levels in the south, attention from visitors is primarily focussed on the coastline.

Weston-super-Mare emerged as an affluent resort in the late-Victorian era, boasting sandy beaches and the aptly-named headland, Sand Point. Two piers were built to entertain visitors and the town thrived.

However, with the advent of the package holiday, more people went abroad for their holidays and the town, like many of the UK's seaside resorts, struggled to maintain visitor numbers.

The coast at Weston still attracts millions of day visitors each year, boasting attractions including a helicopter museum, Weston-super-Mare Museum, the Grand Pier and the SeaQuarium aquarium.

In August 2015, Weston hosted the Dismaland temporary installation by artist Banksy.

Clevedon, north of Weston, is a somewhat more relaxed neighbour, with ornamental gardens and a Victorian bandstand marking the seafront.

It is surrounded by hills, providing stunning views of the North Somerset coastline, including at Church Hill and Wain's Hill, which is topped by the remains of an Iron Age hill fort. The coast continues northwards, to places such as Portishead, dating back as far as Roman times the town is referred to in the Domesday Book as Portsheve. It's name derives from the 'port at the head of the river' and the town grew around its fishing port and its 19th Century docks.

Venture inland and North Somerset offers some relatively unknown gems, including the National Trust-run Tyntesfield estate, Clevedon Court and the Mendip Hills, as well as the limestone gorge at Burrington Combe and the town of Nailsea.

in association with

WILKIE MAY & TUCKWOOD

www.wilkie.co.uk

The seafront at Weston-super-Mare draws millions of visitors each year

The Jubilee Clock Tower in Churchill, built in 1897

did you know?

- Owing to the large tidal range in the Bristol Channel, the low tide mark in Weston Bay is about a mile from the seafront.

- Much of the TV series Broadchurch was filmed in and around Clevedon and visitors can follow a Broadchurch Trail, taking in many of the locations.

- Actor and comedian John Cleese was born in Weston-super-Mare in 1939.

- Frederick Weatherly, who wrote the lyrics to Danny Boy and Roses of Picardy, was born in Portishead in 1848.

- Weston-super-Mare was home to several war industries and was bombed by the Luftwaffe between 1940 and 1942.

- Isambard Kingdom Brunel and his family lived in Weston-super-Mare while he was supervising the construction of the Bristol and Exeter Railway.

- Poet Alfred Tennyson was a visitor to Clevedon and is among those commemorated in Poets Walk.

- On January 2, 1900, B.C. Hucks became the first aviator to fly a plane across the Bristol Channel, travelling from Weston Airfield to Cardiff and back in a Blackburn monoplane.

- Built in 1894, the Black Nore Lighthouse at Portishead, was decommissioned on September 29, 2010.

- On July 28, 2008, the pavilion at the end of the Grand Pier in Weston-super-Mare was completely destroyed by fire.

- Deep Purple guitarist Ritchie Blackmore was born in Weston-super-Mare in April 1945.

- Clevedon is home to the Curzon cinema, the oldest purpose-built cinema in the world which is still in working order.

- The Dismaland exhibition, by street artist Banksy, is estimated to have brought 150,000 visitors to Weston-super-Mare when it was in situ between August and September 2015.

The gardens at the Tyntesfield Estate, near Clevedon

A distinctive building in the village of Banwell (left)

■ A quiet sunny scene in Barton (left)

■ Christon, one of North Somerset's most picturesque villages (below)

Cyclists and walkers enjoy the Winscombe Strawberry Line (main image); looking across the hills near Loxton (top left); the picturesque approach to Loxton (top right)

north somerset

■ The Gothic St Peter's Church in Portishead (right) was Grade 1 Listed in 1952

■ The 'When Shall We Three Meet Again?' sculpture by Robert Stuart Clamp at Portishead Marina

Sculpture commemorating the importation of phosphorus at Portishead, at the marina

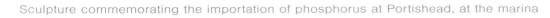

Michael Dan Archer's sweeping nautical artwork 'Full Fathom Five', remembering seafarers and Portishead's nautical history

Vessels moored at Portishead Quays

Embelishments at Tyntesfield House (main image); the gothic house (top right); stonework frames a view of the stunning gardens at Tyntesfield (bottom right)

Pictures: Paul Jones

Reflective waters on the seafront at Clevedon

Weston-super-Mare's landmark pier seen from the seafront promenade

The Grand Pier at Weston, rebuilt after a severe fire in 2008 at a cost of 39 million pounds, reopened on October 23, 2010

mendip

bohemian culture, england's 'smallest city' and a legendary arthurian landscape

The relatively small population of the Mendip area hides an enormous wealth of culture, history and beauty.

Although a largely rural district, it boasts many world-leading qualities in a range of fields.

It is home to the city of Wells, often referred to as 'England's smallest city', although it has a population greater than that of the City of London.

The stunning Wells Cathedral and Bishop's Palace pull visitors to the heart of the city, where the compact nature of the development means tourists can become truly immersed in the history around each corner.

Not far away is Glastonbury, a burgeoning bastion of bohemian culture combined with a wealth of truly historic religious landmarks, including the Abbey and of course,

perhaps Somerset's most famous spectacle, the Tor.

A source of confusion for many, the Tor is actually the hill itself, with the iconic structure on top, the 14th Century St Michael's Tower, built by the Abbot Adam of Sodbury as part of a larger church, which was destroyed during the dissolution of the monasteries in 1539.

Many believe the site is the location of Avalon, from Arthurian legend, leading to the area being known as the Vale of Avalon.

Nearby, of course, is Pilton, home to Michael Eavis' Worthy Farm where the Glastonbury Festival of Contemporary Performing Arts is staged, while the Bath and West showground is also close by.

Shepton Mallet epitomises everything Somerset. Famed for its cider production, the town features some largely-unknown parks

with stunning views of the River Sheppey, including Kilver Court Gardens.

Frome too features a myriad of scenic spots for the visitor to enjoy.

Surrounding the towns is the trademark Somerset landscape of rolling hills combined with the flat marshland of the Levels.

For an unusual look at the county, visitors can venture into the plethora of caves under the Mendip Hills, home to the largest underground river system in Britain.

in association with

www.wilkie.co.uk

A view across the Mendips from Walton Hill

A view from a lookout point at Dear Leap near the village of Priddy

did you know?

■ Glastonbury has long been at the centre of a story which claims Jesus visited the town, along with Joseph of Arimathea. However, research concluded the story not to be true, claiming it was probably a construct to encourage profitable pilgrimages to the town abbey.

■ The city of Wells is used as the fictional town of Sandford, Gloucestershire, in the film Hot Fuzz. Co-writer and director of the film, Edgar Wright, grew up in the city.

■ Formula One driver and former world champion, Jenson Button, was born in Frome and still has family in the area.

■ With around 170,000 people on site, the Glastonbury Festival of Contemporary Performing Arts more than doubles the population of the Mendip district (around 112,000).

■ Cider production at Shepton Mallet stretches back more than 200 years, with brands including Blackthorn, Olde English and Gaymers produced at the cider mill. However, production was due to end in 2016, although fruit will still be pulped at the Somerset mill.

■ Archaeologists believe the Chalice Well at Glastonbury has been in use for at least 2,000 years.

■ Ebbor Gorge is a limestone gorge designated and notified in 1952 as a 63.5-hectare biological Site of Special Scientific Interest.

■ Frome is believed to have at least one system of underground tunnels beneath older parts of the town, although their purpose - and true length - is unknown.

■ The Society of Friends established itself in Street in the mid-17th century. Among them was the Clark family, including brothers Cyrus and James, who together founded and developed what is today known as the Clark's shoe maker and has its headquarters on the outskirts of the village.

■ The entrance to the Church of St John The Baptist in Frome features a stone-sculptured Via Crucis (Way of the Cross), which was formed during the mid-19th Century by Rev William James Early Bennett and carved by James Forsyth depicting the journey of Jesus to the Cross.

Sheep grazing at the foot of the Glastonbury Tor

mendip

■ Free range eggs on sale in Priddy (top left)

■ Hurdles at Priddy, formally used as pens for the Priddy Sheep Fair. Legend says, if they ever go, the sheep fair will not be held again (below)

The wind whistles through a field at Priddy (right)

The Ribbon Tower, in the Park area of the Glastonbury Festival, provides stunning views of the site (main image); the festival's iconic Pyramid Stage (inset)

Pictures: Paul Jones

The Glastonbury Tor and the Mendips stand tall above the Levels

mendip

■ A piece from the Via Crucis at St John the Baptist Church in Frome (top left)

■ The ornamental Frome/Selwood clock in the town centre (bottom left)

Frome's St John the Baptist Church (main image)

The stream winding down Cheap Street in Frome

■ A view of the Glastonbury Tor from Walton Hill (top left)

■ The moon rises over the Glastonbury plains (right)

St Michael's Church tower on the Tor (above)

People visit the iconic Glastonbury Tor all year round

■ A wood sculpture at Ebbor Gorge (top left)

■ A plaque commemorating the donation of the land to the National Trust (inset)

EBBOR GORGE AND SURROUNDING WOODLAND
WERE GIVEN TO THE NATIONAL TRUST BY
MRS. G.W. HODGKINSON, IN MEMORY OF,
THE RT HON. SIR WINSTON CHURCHILL,
K.G., O.M., C.H., T.D.
THIS STONE WAS UNVEILED BY
HIS GRAND-DAUGHTER, MRS. PIERS DIXON
ON 17TH MAY, 1967.

Ebbor Gorge covers 157 acres

A view across Mendip from Ebbor

mendip

- The historic Market Cross in Shepton Mallet (top left)
- The view up The Batch, Shepton Mallet (bottom left)

St Peter's Church in Evercreech (right)

Flags flying high after the sun has gone down in Street

Wells Cathedral, which sits at the heart of 'England's smallest city'

The walls surrounding the Bishop's Palace, Wells, which feature heavily in the comedy film, Hot Fuzz

north east somerset

a world heritage city, historic architecture, market towns and stunning scenery

Featuring rolling hills and river valleys, the district of Bath and North Somerset has it all. At its heart, of course, lies Bath, a World Heritage City.

Famed for its waters in Georgian times, Bath itself bathes in the splendour of the era, with stunning architecture at every turn.

Combined with a thriving arts and culture scene, it has plenty to offer.

However, covering an area of 136 square miles, two thirds of the district is green belt - and the surrounding scenery is as enthralling as the administrative centre.

There are picturesque villages aplenty on offer, including the traditional market towns of Keynsham and Midsummer Norton, as well as the Chew Valley.

For those wishing to venture beyond Bath's city boundaries, there is also much to see in towns and villages along the River Chew, including Chew Magna, Stanton Drew, Compton Dando and Chewton Keynsham.

Chew Magna in particular boasts a wealth of Listed buildings, despite a number of German bombs falling on the parish during the Second World War.

Pillboxes from World War Two remain visible in areas to the north of the village.

The River Somer flows through the heart of Midsomer Norton and was prone to flooding.

A major tunnel, completed in 1977, was built beneath the High Street to prevent serious flooding.

At Keynsham, the Roman influence is particularly prominent, with two Roman villas discovered in the area, alongside at least 15 other buildings beneath Keynsham Hams.

Meanwhile, the importance of mining to the area is highlighted in Radstock, which has a winding wheel and headframe on display outside the Radstock Museum, where coal was discovered around 1763.

After a boom in the industry – and in the area as a result – complex geology made extracting the coal difficult.

The industry declined and the district's last two mines, Kilmersdon and Writhlington, closed in 1973.

in association with

www.wilkie.co.uk

A barge sailing at Saltford

Chew Valley Lake is surrounded by villages steeped in history

did you know?

The population of Bath and North East Somerset is around 170,000. Approximately half live in the City of Bath - making it 12 times more densely populated than the rest of the area.

Prior to Chew Magna coming into being, the manor of Chew was held by the Bishops of Bath and Wells from 1062 to 1548, and was called Chew Episcopi or Bishop's Chew.

Keynsham was home to Cadbury's Somerdale production plant and produced popular snacks such as the Double Decker, Cream Eggs and Dairy Milk. It was closed in 2011 with production moving to Poland.

More than 15 Roman buildings have been detected beneath the Keynsham Hams.

The bishops built a palace near the Church of St Andrews, which was visited by Henry III in 1250. Chew Court is a surviving part of the palace.

Children's author Roald Dahl used to sell kerosene in Midsomer Norton and the surrounding area in the 1930s.

Contrary to popular belief, the TV series Midsomer Murders is not filmed in Midsomer Norton, nor is it based on the town. The name was borrowed from the town by writer Anthony Horowitz when he adapted Caroline Graham's Chief Inspector Barnaby series for television in 1997.

The 2002 World Professional Billiards Championship was held at the Centurion Hotel in Midsomer Norton.

Bath attracts around 7 million day visits each year, with tourism employing an estimated 11,800 people.

Bath hosted the first ever farmers' market in 1987.

The Circus in Bath is the same diameter as Stonehenge.

William James Blacker, a prominent Australian politician representing the Liberal and Democratic Union in the South Australian House of Assembly from 1892 to 1902, was born in Radstock.

The spoil heap of Writhlington Colliery, near Radstock, is now a Site of Special Scientific Interest where more than 1,400 insect fossil specimens have been recovered.

The sunset captured near Bath

Trees silhouetted by the setting sun at Keynsham

The rural outlook at Keynsham

The village of Saltford boasts a marina (right) and is home to the Avon County Rowing Club and walks or cycleways along the River Avon

Wheels within wheels at Market Walk, Keynsham

Memorial Park, Keynsham (main image); corn fields in the distance near Bath (top right); Signposts at St Mary's Church, West Harptree (bottom right)

St Michael's Church towers over Compton Martin

north east somerset

■ Bath Abbey is the centrepiece of tours which take in the wealth of architectural gems on offer in the city (below)

Bath Abbey's West Front, with unique Ladders of Angels (right)

The Pulteney Bridge, built in 1774, is one of just four bridges around the world to have shops lining both sides

north east somerset

- Bath's Royal Crescent (below)
- The Pump Room (top centre)
- Town houses line the many slopes of Bath city centre (bottom left)

Umbrellas form a temporary roof for shoppers in St Lawrence Street, Bath (main image)

Umbrellas form an unusual canopy in St Lawrence Street, Bath

The Royal Crescent, Bath, is among the West Country's most iconic landmarks and ranks among the best examples of Georgian architecture

■ A rugby player shapes up for
a kick in the village of Midsomer
Norton (right)

St John's Church, in Midsomer Norton (above)

St John's Church has seen significant restoration work in recent years

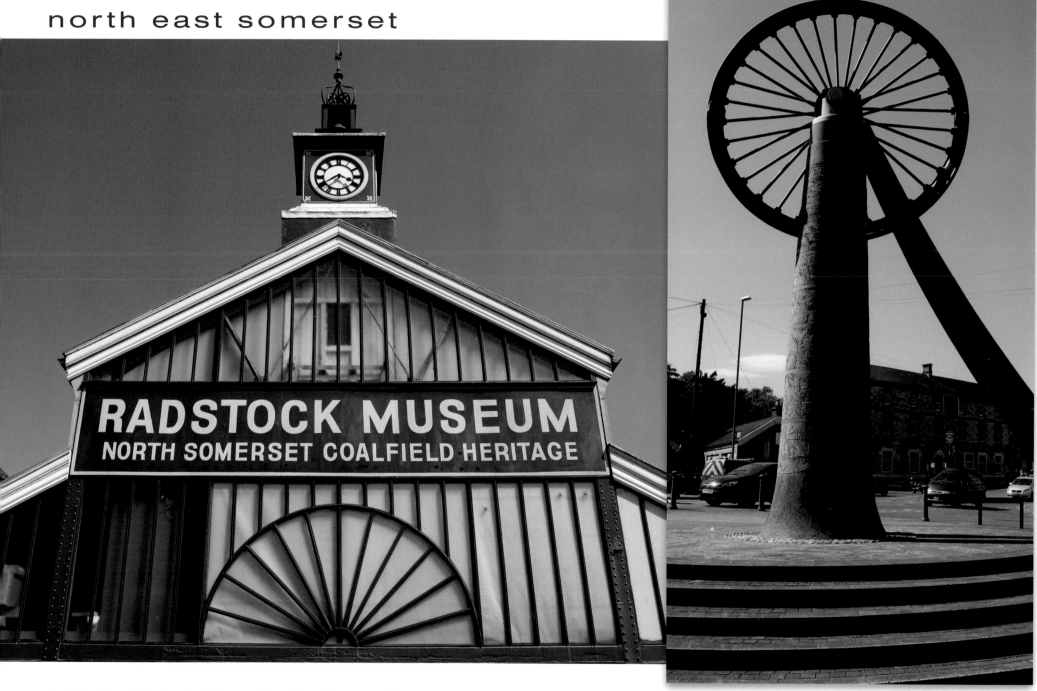

RADSTOCK MUSEUM
NORTH SOMERSET COALFIELD HERITAGE

Radstock is at the heart of the area's mining history and is home to the Radstock Museum, which has a winding wheel and headframe in the Square out front

The war memorial in Radstock

south somerset

a slice of everything somerset, with historic battlefields and charming villages

The defined area of South Somerset is rather misleadingly named. For the district is the largest in England, home to a third of the Somerset population, covering 370 square miles – and includes much of the eastern side of the county. And with such a broad area of interest, it offers the complete spectrum of Somerset life.

From traditional villages such as Combe St Nicholas and Muchelney, to larger towns like Chard, Ilminster and the administrative centre of Yeovil, as well as a sizeable chunk of the Levels, there is an authentic slice of Somerset at every turn.

The district is also home to the historic county town – Somerton – which still carries the grace, historical architecture and underlying confidence of a capital.

Yeovil itself has developed as a centre for the aerospace and defence industries, which led to it being targeted by German bombers during the Second World War.

The Fleet Air Arm still has a base in the town, the primary home of the Royal Navy's Lynx and Sea King helicopters and the Westland Aircraft firm remains among the town's biggest employers.

Crewkerne too has a rich offering of history, showcased at the Crewkerne and District Museum, opened in 2000 at a house with an 18th Century frontage.

Langport, meanwhile, was the venue for a defining moment in the English Civil War when, on July 10 1645, the last effective Royalist field army was defeated and Parliamentary victory became inevitable. The town was also home to a US Army military prison during the Second World War.

Wincanton too has been famed throughout history as the venue of many battles, including between the Britons, Danes and Saxons. During the 19th Century, Wincanton was a depot for French officers during the Napoleonic Wars.

in association with

Signposts near Winsham showcasing the scale of South Somerset

The Church of All Saints rising above Castle Cary

did you know?

■ Chard's branch of the Westminster Bank has an interesting history, as a bomb proof bunker was built behind the branch in 1938 and was used to store copies of bank records, as well as the emergency bank note supply of the Bank of England. There was also speculation the Crown Jewels were stored there.

■ The suburb of Yeoville, in Johannesburg, South Africa, was founded in 1890 by Thomas Yeo Sherwell, a native of Yeovil, Somerset.

■ John Baker, a prominent early Australian politician and the second Premier of South Australia, was born in Ilminster in 1813.

■ Chard suffered serious damage during the English Civil War, particularly in 1644, when Charles I spent a week in the town.

■ Ilminster's Church of St Mary, or The Minster, contains two bells produced by the famous Biblie family, one dating from 1732 and another from 1790.

■ Yeovil's role as a centre for aircraft and defence industry made it the target of bombing during the Second World War. It is still the home of Westland Aircraft.

■ However, Chard is hailed as the birthplace of powered flight after John Stringfellow first demonstrated that engine-powered flight was possible in 1848.

■ Jim Cregan, guitarist with Steve Harley & Cockney Rebel, is a Yeovil native.

■ The majority of dwellings in South Somerset are bungalows, totalling more than 24,000 across the district.

■ South Somerset is made up of 121 parishes, with 102 parish and town councils.

■ In 2006, Yeovil became the first town in Britain to institute a system of biometric fingerprint scanning in nightclubs. It is no longer in operation.

All Saints' Church, in Isle Brewers, which was built in 1861

south somerset

■ The steeply sloping Flingers Lane,
Wincanton (right)

The Bear Inn at the heart of Wincanton High Street

Mist engulfs the lands surrounding Wincanton

south somerset

Cows graze at New House Lodge, near Ilminster (top) which features stunning views of the rural landscape (bottom)

Wincanton's Town Hall with its cheerful summer display of geraniums

south somerset

- The Hood monument at Butleigh stands tall against the summer sky (right)

- The church at Combe St Nicholas has graced the village since Norman times (bottom right)

The Church of St Mary Magdalene in Stowell (main image)

The village of Combe St Nicholas sits on the edge of the picturesque Blackdown Hills

south somerset

■ The thatched former toll house on the A30 near Chard (right)

■ St Mary's Church in Chard (far right)

The rolling hills as seen on the way into Chard (above)

The landmark Guildhall stands in the middle of Chard High Street

south somerset

■ The Stone Circle built in 2000 to commemorate the history of hamstone quarrying here at Ham Hill (top left)

■ A gateway in the village of Martock (right)

■ The war memorial on Ham Hill (top right)

Sculptures at Bruton (bottom left) and in Castle Cary (bottom right)

A walker makes his way up Ham Hill

the levels

mineral-rich and fertile plains, ancient settlements and diverse wildlife

The Somerset Levels – north and south – are bisected by the Polden Hills.

Covering 160,000 acres, the Levels are naturally-formed plains and wetlands, the result of the low-lying, flat landscape, sitting around 20 metres above sea level.

Drained by the Rivers Parrett in the south and in the north by the Axe and Brue, the land has been exploited for minerals for centuries.

Settlements dating back to the Neolithic period have been discovered on raised land – notably at Brent Knoll and Glastonbury – with wooden trackways used to extract minerals, including sea salt, during Roman times.

The uniqueness of the environment brings with it some important wildlife and rich biodiversity and the Levels include 32 Sites of Special Scientific Interest.

Species including Bewick's swan, Eurasian curlew, the marsh harrier and peregrine falcon all feed in the area.

Man-made efforts to drain the Levels were documented in the Domesday Book, with monasteries at Glastonbury, Athelney and Muchelney behind much of the work.

During the Second World War, the artificial Huntspill River was constructed as a reservoir.

The Sowy River between the River Parrett and King's Sedgemoor Drain was completed in 1972 and water levels are managed by the Levels internal drainage boards.

In January 2014, a major incident was declared after storms had seen 17,000 acres of the Levels underwater for more than a month.

The flooding has seen the reintroduction of dredging to rivers in the region, as well as major improvements to the flood control systems.

Farming makes up much of today's use of the Levels, including willow, an industry recognised by the construction of the Willow Man sculpture near Bridgwater and the Willow Cathedral in Taunton.

in association with

WILKIE MAY & TUCKWOOD

www.wilkie.co.uk

A view across the Levels from near Combe Hill Wood

The view from Swell

did you know?

■ While notable floods took place on the Levels in 1703, 1872 and as recently as 2013/14, the worst in recorded history were during the Bristol Channel floods of 1607, which resulted in the drowning of an estimated 2,000 or more people.

■ An economic impact assessment showed the 2013/14 winter floods cost the county up to £147 million.

■ The landscape of the Levels is 70 per cent grassland, 30 per cent arable.

■ King Alfred the Great lived on the Levels.

■ In September 1998, cousins Kevin and Martin Elliott discovered a hoard of Roman coins at Shapwick. Featuring 9,238 silver Roman coins, some dating from 31-30 BC, the find was the second largest from the time of the Roman Empire. It is now on display at the Museum of Somerset, in Taunton.

■ In times gone by, Brent Knoll was known as the Isle or Mount of Frogs, with legend saying Ider son of Nuth, one of King Arthur's knights, went to the mount on a quest to slay three giants who lived there.

■ Humans are believed to have inhabited the Levels for more than 500,000 years. A Palaeolithic flint tool found in Westbury is the earliest indication of human presence.

■ The best-preserved prehistoric village in the UK, Glastonbury Lake Village, was discovered in 1892 by Arthur Bulleid. It was inhabited by about 200 people living in 14 roundhouses.

■ The Levels are home to the largest lowland population of breeding wading birds in the UK.

■ The Levels were regularly flooded by sea water at high tide, which was not prevented until the early 20th century, when improved sea defences were installed.

■ Willow from the Levels is used to create artist charcoal, notably by the Coate family, in Stoke St Gregory.

A pylon sits in a field at Clavelshay

A tractor at work in Tarnock

Flooding on the Levels

Flood waters at Othery (left and right)

Flooded farmland around Burrowbridge

■ Cattle enjoying the views of the River Huntspill at West Huntspill (left)

The man-made River Huntspill, which was built in 1940 to supply water to Royal Ordnance Factory Bridgwater

A murmuration of starlings at the end of another day above the Levels

the levels

A view of the River Sowy from the Blind Man's Gate Bridge (main image)

The summer sun slowly setting over Steart Marshes

Bales of hay neatly arranged at Green Ore, near Wells

A picturesque view from Basin Bridge, near Highbridge

Electricity cables trace the horizon as the sun sets over the Levels

Looking to the coast from Treborough, on Exmoor

west somerset

a heritage railway, chocolate-box villages and the south west coastal path

Covering an area of 740 square miles, West Somerset's population of just over 35,000 makes it the least populace non-unitary district in England.

The rural status of the area means it is home to a wide variety of spectacular landscapes. Almost two-thirds of the western half of the district is part of Exmoor National Park and boasts a large number of Listed buildings in a host of scenic towns and villages. While in the east, the Quantock Hills lead inland to Taunton Deane.

Dunster Castle overlooks the village of the same name, which itself contains the beautiful Yarn Market and Gallox Bridge.

Down the road is Minehead, the largest town in the district, famed as a holiday destination and home to a large Butlins resort, opened in 1962.

The town sits at the foot of North Hill, which offers stunning views of the coast and scenery dominated by bell heather and bracken and is home to unusual birds such as the Dartford warbler.

Walkers can also venture along the South West Coast Path National Trail, which begins in Minehead, and hope to see the famous Exmoor ponies which roam the landscape.

In nearby Watchet, visitors can take in the scenic marina and in the centre of the Esplanade, iconic statues of The Ancient Mariner and Yankee Jack by the renowned Scottish artist, Alan Herriot.

Move along the coast in either direction and more scenic locations are revealed, including Porlock and Blue Anchor.

Tarr Steps, near Dulverton, a clapper bridge across the River Barle, dates from around 1000BC.

Continuing the journey inland, the district is home to many picturesque villages, including Williton, Stogumber, Nether Stowey and Bishops Lydeard.

The West Somerset Railway - the longest steam-powered heritage railway in the country - runs through most of the district, from Bishop's Lydeard in the south east, to Minehead in the north west and a trip along the line gives a complete resume of the varied and enthralling vistas on offer.

in association with

www.wilkie.co.uk

A view from the road between Porlock and Lynmouth

did you know?

■ The Quantock Hills became the first Area of Outstanding Natural Beauty created in the UK in 1956.

■ Arthur C. Clarke, author of 2001: A Space Odyssey, lived in Minehead.

■ At Porlock Beach, during low tide, the remains of a submerged forest can be seen. The area was inland until the sea level in the Bristol Channel rose between 7,000 and 8,000 years ago.

■ According to the Office for National Statistics in 2009, the population of West Somerset has the oldest average age in the United Kingdom, at 52.

■ Tarr Steps, a clapper bridge construction, is constructed from stone slabs weighing up to two tons each. Legend has it they were installed by the devil to win a bet.

■ Minehead is the starting point of the South West Coast Path National Trail, the nation's longest long-distance countryside walking trail.

■ Mathematician and pioneer of the computer, Ada Lovelace, used Worthy Manor, in Ashley Combe, as a summer retreat.

■ The West Somerset Railway is the longest standard gauge independent heritage railway in the United Kingdom, at 22.75 miles long.

■ Samuel Taylor Coleridge, who lived at Nether Stowey, was interrupted while writing Kubla Khan by 'a person from Porlock', and never finished the poem.

■ Cecil Frances Alexander wrote the hymn All Things Bright And Beautiful in Minehead and Dunster.

■ Watchet Harbour became the inspiration for Samuel Taylor Coleridge's poem, The Ancient Mariner, after a walk with friends William and Dorothy Wordsworth from his home in Nether Stowey across the Quantocks in 1797.

■ English author Richard Doddridge Blackmore's Lorna Doone, published in 1869, was based on a true story and Oare Church was the scene of Lorna's death.

■ The A39 road up Porlock Hill boasts a 1-in-4 gradient and hairpin bends! The steep incline is avoidable, however, by using a toll road.

Stunning coastline at Blue Anchor

west somerset

■ Wildflowers on Exmoor (below)

■ An Exmoor pony silhouetted against the coastline in West Somerset (bottom)

Exmoor ponies enjoying the scenery (main image)

Picture: Simon Billing (main image)

The view from Porlock Hill up the Bristol Channel towards the Islands of Flat Holm and Steep Holm, Weston-super-Mare beyond, and a distant Welsh coast on the left

west somerset

■ Stones on Bossington Beach
(top right)

■ A view from the Porlock toll road
(bottom right)

Waterfalls at St Audries Bay (left and top centre)

Picture: Malcolm Lewis (bottom right)

The coast at St Audries Bay

The Lookout Point at Dunkery Beacon, where sightseers include grazing sheep

Dunkery Beacon looking towards the sea

west somerset

■ The Minehead skyline is dominated at one end by North Hill (right and below)

■ Walk of art... the start of the South West Coastal Path is marked by a large sculpture on Minehead's seafront

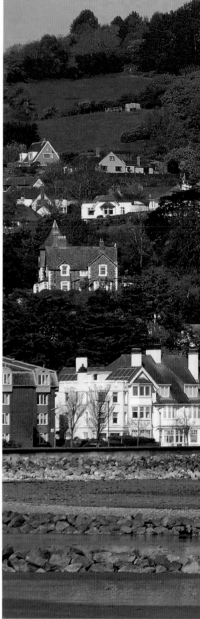

Houses overlooking the seafront at Minehead

west somerset

- A 'chocolate-box' Dunster scene (left)
- Gallox Bridge (centre)
- The Yarn Market roof in Dunster Village with Dunster Castle beyond (bottom left)

Dunster Castle, former refuge of Charles I (right)

A view from West Quantoxhead looking across the Brendon hills, Exmoor and North Hill

west somerset

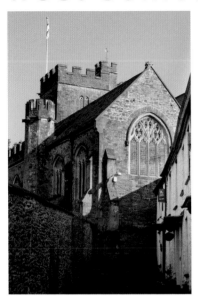

■ All Saints Church, Dulverton (top left)

■ The Lorna Doone statue in Dulverton (below)

The Parish Chruch of St George in Sampford Brett (main image)

The bridge crossing the River Barle at Dulverton

Getting close to sunset at Doniford Beach

west somerset

Watchet Harbour wall and lighthouse (above) and the town's Ancient Mariner statue (right)

Tarr Steps, near Dulverton, in use today as they have been for possibly 3,000 years

coastline

picture-perfect coastal scenery, tranquil beaches and bustling tourist hotspots

From the calming landscapes of Brean Sands or Kilve, to the more lively holiday resorts of Weston-super-Mare and Burnham-on-Sea, Somerset's coastline is a varied and enthralling offering.

More than 36 million visits were made to Somerset in 2015 - many of them heading for the coast.

Families enjoying the sand and sea at Butlins in Minehead are minutes away from the busy working harbour at Watchet, while Hinkley Point is home to operational nuclear power stations, the scale of the developments sitting in stark contrast to the pretty understatement of nearby Portishead harbour.

The tidal waters move in and out, constantly revealing new views of some of the UK's most beautiful coastline.

Away from the resorts, the coastline offers stunning vistas at Exmoor and beyond, ideal for walkers and visitors looking for that perfect photo opportunity.

From Porlock Weir to Brean, the Grand Pier at Weston to the quiet beach at Blue Anchor and the sheer beauty of Clevedon, Somerset's coastline boasts a range of industry and a host of attractions for visitors and residents alike.

Porlock's oyster farm is now operating, while Berrow boasts an award-winning beach complete with shipwreck and sand dunes.

Contrast Sand Point, near Weston, where the Levels meet the sea, with the dramatic cliffs at Exmoor and the peaceful retreats inbetween and it is easy to see why the county's coast has proved so inspirational for the likes of poet Samuel Taylor Coleridge and author Arthur C Clarke.

And those looking to get active during their time on the coast can also enjoy excellent opportunities for kite flying, picnics and the chance to spot some stunning wildlife.

Whether you desire time to reflect, savour the wonders of nature, or enjoy a lively seaside break, the Somerset coast showcases the best of British.

in association with

The base of North Hill at Minehead Harbour at sunset

Sunlight breaches the clouds over Hinkley Point

did you know?

- The estuary of the River Parrett where it flows into the Bristol Channel, near Burnham-on-Sea, has the second highest tidal range in the world at 11 metres (36 ft), second only to the Bay of Fundy in Eastern Canada.

- The beach at Kilve is a Site of Special Scientific Interest, featuring spectacular rock formations and is popular among geologists and visitors searching for fossils.

- In 1897 Guglielmo Marconi, the inventor of the wireless, successfully transmitted radio signals across the Bristol Channel from Penarth to Brean Down.

- Banksy's Dismaland installation, at Weston, saw celebrities including Brad Pitt, Jack Black and Russell Brand visit the town, along with 150,000 others, boosting the economy in Weston-super-Mare by an estimated £20 million.

- The Burnham-on-Sea Area Rescue Boat Search and Rescue (BARB) boat house, on the sea front, was built in 1994 by the Challenge Anneka TV show.

- In 2001, tourism in Somerset was estimated to support around 23,000 people.

- Burnham-on-Sea's first lifeboat was provided in 1836 by the Corporation of Bridgwater.

- The islands in the Bristol Channel technically 'belong' to Cardiff.

- The 37-mile coastline of Exmoor National Park features the highest in England and Wales, with coastal hills rising to 433 metres at Culbone Hill. The highest sheer cliff is 244 metres, on Great Hangman, the highest sea cliff in England and Wales.

- The old Chantry at Kilve beach, founded in 1329, was once used for storing barrels of smuggled spirits.

- The beach running between Burnham and Brean is the second longest stretch of sand in Europe.

- It is possible to walk along the coast from Minehead to Bristol – although you do come inland along the River Parrett to Bridgwater and back out to Weston-super-Mare.

Rock formations at St Audries Bay

coastline

A sign pointing to the beach at Bossington (top left) Bossington Beach scenes (top right & bottom left); boats sit idle at Porlock Weir (right)

Picture: Madeline Taylor (bottom right)

Masts rise into the sky at sunset at Porlock Weir Harbour

Minehead boasts a scenic harbour (top left, top centre and right) and sits at the foot of North Hill (bottom left)

The Balmoral docks at Minehead Harbour

coastline

A bird pokes its head out at the Chantry (top left); Kilve (bottom left, centre and right) boasts amazing rock formations and is visible at St Audries Bay (top right)

Eroded structures blend into the natural furniture at St Audries Bay

Blue Anchor offers stunning coastal views (top and bottom left); The Mariner Statue looks over proceedings in Watchet (right)

Berrow Beach awaiting visitors for the summer season

coastline

Burnham-on-Sea is a haven for wildlife and tourists

The wooden lighthouse on Burnham-on-Sea Beach awaits an approaching storm

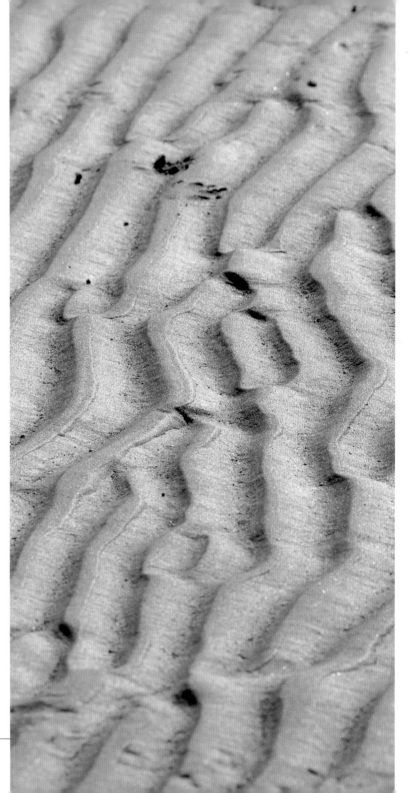

Dog walkers on the shore at Burnham-on-Sea as sands echo the approaching storm

The sun breaches storm clouds over Burnham-on-Sea

Brean Sands boasts a raft of walks for visitors and residents

The Victorian Pier at Clevedon was opened in 1869

coastline

- A tree shaped by sea winds at Brean Down (top left)
- The natural power of the sun beams down on the nuclear facility at Hinkley Point (right)

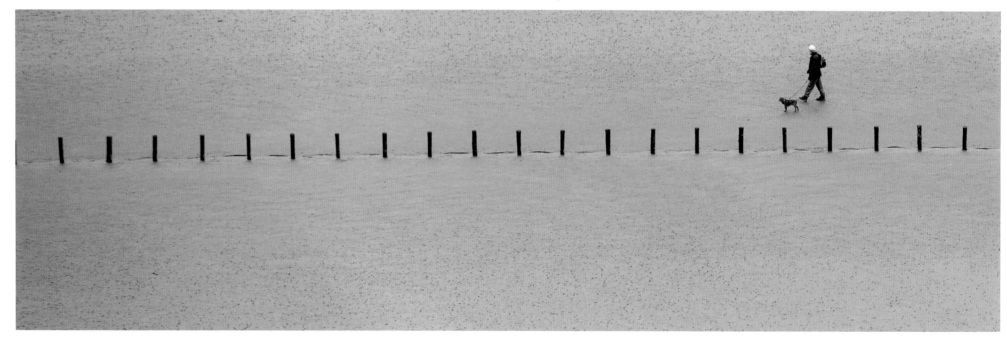

A dog walker makes his way across Brean Beach (bottom)

Ponies have been brought in to help clear unwanted vegetation at Brean Down to allow native wild plants to grow

coastline

Weston-super-Mare has been a tourist hotspot since Victorian times

who did what

pictures: All pictures not credited were taken by Aisling Magill and Steve Richardson.

Thank you to the readers, credited at the bottom of pages featuring their photographs, who took the time to submit so many fantastic images. Sadly, we could not include them all.

design and layout: John Nesbitt, James Barham

words and picture research: Paul Jones

picture captions: Paul Jones, Liz Bond, John Nesbitt

production: Pauline White, Liz Bond

book sales: Pauline White - 01823 365209

published by

Somerset's heartbeat since 1836
County Gazette
www.countygazette.co.uk

in association with

WILKIE MAY & TUCKWOOD

The region's premier independent estate agents
www.wilkie.co.uk

printed by:
Westdale Press Ltd of Cardiff
www.westdale.co.uk

somerset

picture this...

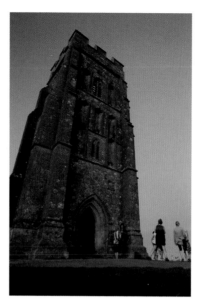

Staff-taken pictures in this book are available to purchase in a range of print sizes and styles.

If you would like to order prints either:

■ Call in to the County Gazette office at 44 St James Street, Taunton TA1 1JR and fill in an order form

■ Visit www.countygazette.co.uk/photosales

Published by Newsquest (South West) Ltd,
St James Street,
Taunton
TA1 1JR

First published in 2016

ISBN 0-9933533-6-9

Picture: Paul Jones (bottom left)